Tender Fractures: The Bittersweet Dance of Feminine Love and Self

Payton Sivak

India | USA | UK

Presentation by *BookLeaf Publishing*

Web: www.bookleafpub.com

E-mail: info@bookleafpub.com

ISBN: 9789363309753

First edition 2024

ACKNOWLEDGEMENT

I wish to express my heartfelt gratitude to all who have shown me love throughout my life. To my family and friends, your unwavering support has been a guiding light. To those who are no longer with us, including past partners and dear friends, your impact remains profound. Each of you has helped me cultivate a deeper understanding of true love and companionship, enriching my life in ways I will forever cherish. Thank you for being a vital part of my story.

PREFACE

To write and to speak are among the greatest gifts of human existence. Creating art with a higher purpose allows us to give voice to those whose mouths have been woven shut, to the experiences and words that have been blurred. Reflecting on my own hidden experiences, kept beneath the surface of my subconscious, I have expressed myself through various forms of art.

Love is both beautiful and injurious. To love is a profound ability that transcends people and emotional landscapes. Being female and navigating femininity brings about a distinct kind of love, accompanied by heart-wrenching scenarios that reflect the complexities of relationships.

I aim to explore the underlying psyche of love—the rarely discussed, often overlooked aspects. I want to speak for those lovers who struggle to find their own words, for women who cannot articulate their feelings. I will do this through a collection of poems. My hope is to connect with readers' inner consciousness through the power of words, offering understanding and companionship through my own experiences. Enjoy.

Birth

My being, a vessel profound,
necessary to humanity's ground.

My seed, a font of potent might,
not to be discarded,
abused,
relied.

For I am the root of the world's expanse,
my consciousness assembles, in cosmic dance.

To Make a House a Home

To my dearest,
for the walls I built within us,
strong as historic wood, shielding us from the
storm outside,
cultivating a refuge from humanity's chaos and
strife.

The love within my heart, flowing like a stream
to yours,
nourishing and fostering every tender attack.

To keep the house tidy, like a garden in full
glory,
the clothes washed,
soft and fresh as spring rain;
My babies fed,
warm and satisfied as the morning sun.

And no matter my abilities,
no matter the challenges,
It is all for you.

For in the end, it was never truly my home

Ghost in the Daylight

Love is a ghost that haunts the spaces between
breaths,
a whisper in the dark corners of our souls,
where shadows cling and memories linger.
It is the ache in the pit of our stomachs,
a silent promise made in the midst of chaos.

We chase it like a fading dream,
grasping at its elusive form as it slips through
our fingers.
Love is the quiet storm that drowns out reason,
the fever that burns in our veins,
a longing that defies explanation.

In your eyes, I see a reflection of the past,
a thousand nights spent tracing constellations,
searching for meaning in the stars.
Yet love remains a distant, flickering light,
a beacon that guides us through the fog of
uncertainty.

We build our hopes on fragile wings,
praying they won't break under the weight of
our fears.
Love is the soft touch we crave in the dark,

a balm for our wounded hearts,
a solace found in the spaces we share.

But as the dawn breaks and the shadows retreat,
we are left with echoes of what was,
a memory of a love that burned too brightly,
leaving only traces in its wake,
a reminder of the ghost we once chased.

Beneath the Moon's Edge

Standing just a foot away from the lake,
I feel the bitter chill that winter makes.
With a single step, the ice will break;
the moon will fall into the wide, frozen wake.

Kneeling, I tap, questioning the strength of the
ice.
He, the moon, responds with webs of cracks,
an indication of slight durability;
with an echoing resound of the night,
he calls upon me, "Come child, this way—
play under the moon of midnight."

I step back, for the ice and moon draw me
nearer;
an incentive of freedom. The chill will shoot
through my body
as I plummet into the moon's craters.
Perhaps I will finally feel, perhaps I will be free
to dance under the stars. At last, we shall be
together.

As he entered the lake, surrounded by a divine
aura,
his presence captivated me.

Like the sun emerging from behind a cloudy
veil,
casting an ethereal brightness that illuminated
the night.
With star-like eyes, twinkling with a brilliance
that reflected the constellations above,
drawing you in like a sailor navigating by distant
galaxies.
Time seemed to stop, leaving only the echoes
of the universe's eternal love song.

Our little hamlet was swiftly plunged into
winter's gloom,
the lake frozen over once more. The forest
encased in snow,
reaching the water's edge. Those who reach the
moon
won't want to come back down.

In the final phase of the moon's lunar cycle,
amidst the waning light of December's dusk,
ensnared in a moment of fateful decision,
heeding the whispered entreaties of the celestial
orb above,
he ventured too far onto the fragile surface of the
ice.
In that precarious moment, suspended between
solid ground and the abyss below,

he confronted a choice that would alter his life's
course.

The ice groaned beneath his weight, threatening
to release its grip.
He stayed, a silent supplicant to the whims of
fate.
With eyes closed against the harsh reality of his
predicament,
he surrendered to the moon's radiant call.
Its luminous beams wove a mesmerizing
tapestry,
coaxing him closer to oblivion.

He wished to die, the moon's light so pure,
its web of cracks became a lure.
He fell, trapped under ice's spell,
disappeared where shadows dwell.
At Everest's base, he looked up high,
at the moon, a distant sky.

And so I stand, near the frozen lake,
winter's chill making my body ache.
I step on ice, see my scarred eyes,
reflecting the moon, a solemn prize.
He shines as brightly as before,
the last light in the frozen forest's core.

He's smiling, he sways and so I reach.

I put the moon's head into my pocket and shine.
The dead dark moon's night sky falls, and so do
I.
Spinning, my collapsed body falls from the
surface
with the same frozen eyes.

I can't hear anything, I can't touch anything, I
can't move but I can still see.
Spinning, this painful trembling kindly lets me
sleep.
In the night sky, I bid farewell to the broken you.
I turn to the stars. I crumble and fall apart as the
moon descends into the open hole.
Together forever, under the transparent night, we
shine as stars.

In the celestial expanse, I say my goodbyes to
your shattered form.
I shift my gaze to the glittering constellations.
I disintegrate,
collapsing as the moon descends into the abyss.
At last, we are eternally entwined beneath the
crystal-clear night.
We radiate as stars.
Beside the celestial river of the Galaxy,
our unity is eternal.

Luminous Drowning

A sight I first thought beautiful,
the moon resting close to my being,
its prisms lighting up the night sky, outshining
any star with a soft cry.
And with the moon's mirrored light,
all celestial beings were left distorted,
twisted into a curved wave of reflected
nothingness,
like one's warped view upon a body of water.

I wasn't watching the stars slowly sink,
but it was me, the centerpiece of the light,
slowly drowning in the moon's luminous
embrace.

Familiarity

A lover echoes shadows of the past,
recalled and worn like an old cloak.
The absence creates a thirst that cannot be
quenched,
the fear of being found out only ignites the
chase.

Through the trials of exploitation, the true self
reveals itself,
authenticity unfolds amidst the turmoil.
Even under the weight of coercion,
it retains its purity,

it is essential,

it is known,

it is love.

Swan

The angel wings sway in the air,
a momentum, a determination.
The mourning swan flies,
for the feathered plains shake in the distance,
showing a morbid curiosity, preening in mere
excitement.

The branches in a bloviating bewilderment, with
a need to charm,
stretch like eager fingers towards the heavens.

The gray sky, a canvas of sorrow,
welcomes a new companionship,
the clouds dancing in delicate pirouettes.

For a first taste of freedom, the ground begins
inching,
the grass preens to an utmost point,
its green blades glistening with morning dew.

The branches bloviate in preparation,
their leaves rustling like whispered secrets.

The clouds and sky say goodbye,
their edges tinged with the pink of dawn.

And the heavens anticipate,
for the loss remains unbearable.

Our parted necks, forever entangled in harmony,
a silent symphony of yearning.

Love's Beauty

Love is the morning sun warming the cool earth,
a soft touch like silk brushing against bare skin.
It's laughter echoing in golden light,
secrets whispered beneath the shelter of twilight.

In love, we are mirrored in each other's gaze,
our souls intertwining like vines reaching for the
sky.
It's in the tender brush of fingertips,
the way small moments turn into a garden of
warmth.

Love is the scent of rain on dry soil,
the quiet dance of shadows and light.
It transforms the mundane into a canvas of
wonder,
where every glance and touch becomes a
brushstroke of eternity.

Pomegranate

In the heart of a pomegranate lies a mess of
crimson seeds,
each one bursting with the sweetness of hidden
truths.
The fruit's ruby interior, a labyrinth of chaos,
mirrors the tangled beauty of love.

Peeling back its tough skin, you find the juice
staining your fingers,
a vivid reminder of the passion that seeps
through every touch.
Love, too, is a riot of color and mess,
a mosaic of moments that burst and scatter like
seeds.

Each seed holds a story, a fragment of desire,
scattered but whole, a chaotic beauty in its
essence.
The juice, like love, is both messy and rich,
staining the soul with its vibrant intensity.

Just as the pomegranate's splendor emerges from
its disarray,
love finds its form in the tangled, unspoken mess
of the heart.

Both are wild and untamed,
a delicious chaos that makes life exquisitely
unpredictable.

So embrace the mess of the pomegranate,
for within its disordered seeds lies the essence of
what we seek.
In the chaos of love, we find a beauty
that is as rich and profound as the fruit itself.

Despiration

There's a hollow ache in solitude,
no one near to catch the words meant just for
them.
Whispers linger at the edge of my tongue,
words that should bind, perhaps inked in some
forgotten book.

As loneliness deepens, desire sharpens,
yearning twists into a desperate need.
It matters not what fills the emptiness,
only the hunger to be heard, to be seen.

Like a hunger that grows sharper with time,
any word will do, as long as it touches,
as long as it speaks of the ache inside.
In the silence, every word becomes a lifeline,
a fragile bridge over the chasm of longing.

The Man in the Window

What we wish to leave will return in time,
Is it a test or just fate's design?
You've shaped my being, my very essence,
And still, despite your absence, you return.
In different faces, in different tales,
As if the fairytale always rewrites itself.
You linger in the windowpane,
Your anger striking my soul,
The glass piercing my heart,
A pain I cannot ignore.
They were right—once you've shared your life
with a man in the window,
His reflection will haunt you forever.

Voiceless

The words pound in my head, desperate to be
freed,
coursing through my body, burning with need.
Yet, they falter at the base of my throat,
my heartbeat quickens, chasing each unspoken
note.

Pressure builds, my heart frantically insists,
but the words resist, a defiance that persists.
Thoughts flood my mind, relentless in their path,
rushing, colliding, in their desperate wrath.

They clash with my throat, trembling with fear,
wanting to escape, but the thoughts are too near.
Overwhelmed by the force, my heart quakes in
fright,
fear births more thoughts, drowning out the
light.

My words are stifled, too afraid to make a
sound,
in this silent turmoil, I remain eternally bound.

Anonymity and Attachment

With such an absence of individuality, how can
admiration form?
When I am merely a fragment of the universe,
interconnected yet soulless.
What will you do when you see through the
deceit of my persona?
Will your words become mere memories,
vanishing into the infinity of the moon and the
cosmos?
Will you still love me if there has never truly
been a "me"?

I am nearly irreparably damaged.
I offer you my bionic mechanics, desperate for
repair,
they latch onto your core, your essence.
If you leave, you will carry the stitches of my
heart,
and I will be eternally fragmented.

Lush

She looks at her reflection and sees a garden
gone fallow,
the once-lush vines now tangled with thorns of
memory,
each petal lost to hands that promised the moon
but left only shadows in their wake.
Her body, once a symphony of vibrant blooms,
now whispers in a language of wilted leaves and
broken stems.
Each curve, line, and scar is a reminder of stolen
seasons.
She walks through the echo of her own skin.
A ravaged landscape,
where beauty was once a fierce flame,
Is now turned to ashes in the cold light of their
leaving.
They took from her,
not just the bloom,
but the belief that the soil could once again
breathe life into the garden they left behind.
In the hollow of her heart,
where seeds of self-worth lie dormant,
she grieves for the woman who was,
for the lushness that they never tended, only
devoured.

But even in this barren earth,
she senses a stubborn pulse,
a whisper that someday,
even the most desolate garden can be coaxed
back to life.

Lust

Touch me, and I will emerge anew,
a phoenix from the ashes of yesterday's longing.
Kiss me, and I will rise to the heavens,
a soul ascending in the warmth of your desire.
Your longing is a form of love, and my body is
crafted for such yearning,
ripe and ready, an apple hanging low in the
garden of your touch.
I will consume myself in the act of reaching for
you,
devouring the fruit of my own temptation, just to
taste the essence of what you offer.
For even if it leads me to perdition,
I will journey into the depths to savor the
sweetness of your presence.

Monster

A monster hides in the shadows of my room,
its bond to the world severed like a frayed
thread.
She weeps, feeling as though she is nailed shut,
imprisoned by their deceit.
Marked with vileness, her truths twisted into
lies,
But how does one escape the mirror's cruel
distortion when it's the only reflection they've
ever known?

Ambivalence

Upon my skin, your kiss's grace.
In my head, your speech's embrace.
Your interests, now my refuge zone.

Yet your shortcomings, in my thoughts, are
sown.

Your damage etched beneath my skin,
for the impact of your love is everlasting, within

Rewrite

This story can be rewritten, reshaped in our
hands,
you can sink into my car's seat,
your touch no longer lingering on my body,
your words, tender as petals, speaking truths laid
bare.
The fabric of my clothes doesn't hide the past,
but the memory itself fades.
The scars may still be there,
yet we can learn to embrace love, to be gentle.

The shadows of yesterday won't cover the new
lines on my skin,
and you can hold me close once more

www.ingramcontent.com/pod-product-compliance
Lightning Source LLC
LaVergne TN
LVHW021353200726

843509LV00014B/2826